LIFESKILLS IN ACTION

LIVING SKILLS

Finding A Place To Live

CARRIE
GWYNNE

LIFESKILLS IN ACTION

LIVING SKILLS

MONEY

Living on a Budget | Road Trip
Opening a Bank Account | The Guitar
Managing Credit | High Cost
Using Coupons | Get the Deal
Planning to Save | Something Big

LIVING

Smart Grocery Shopping | Shop Smart
Doing Household Chores | Keep It Clean
Finding a Place to Live | A Place of Our Own
Moving In | Pack Up
Cooking Your Own Meals | Dinner Is Served

JOB

Preparing a Résumé
Finding a Job
Job Interview Basics
How to Act Right on the Job
Employee Rights

SADDLEBACK
EDUCATIONAL PUBLISHING
www.sdlback.com

All source images from Shutterstock.com

ISBN-13: 978-1-68021-041-5
ISBN-10: 1-68021-041-6
eBook: 978-1-63078-347-1

Printed in Guangzhou, China
NOR/0116/CA21600020

20 19 18 17 16   1 2 3 4 5

It's time to get a place of your own.

Will it be an apartment?

Or a spare room in a house?

That is up to you.

Finding the right place takes time.

But it's worth it.

It is a big step toward being **independent**.

How do you find a place to live?

First, pick the right area.

Look for places that you like.

Make sure the **rent** is low enough.

Go see places. Fill out forms.

Know what you can afford.

How much do you make each month?

Split it into three parts.

One part can be for rent.

APPLICANT

Last/Family/Sur (Enter name **exactly** as it appears on official documents.)

First/Given

...me, if not first name (only one)

Former last name(s)

...me ○ Home ○ Cell   Home (   )   ○ Female ○ Male

US Social Security Number, if
Required for US Citizens and

mm/dd/yyyy

Area/Country/Ci...

Cell (

Area/Cou...

What about extras?

A pool. A parking spot.

These are nice to have.

But they cost more too.

Think about what you need.

Do you have a bike instead of a car?

Find places close to work or school.

Do you or a roommate have **special needs**?

Look for ramps and first-floor rooms.

Do you have a dog or a cat?

Make sure the place allows pets.

Budget

Income

    Paycheck

Expense

    Rent

    Electric

    Phone

    Grocery

Look at all the **costs**.

Rent. Food. Insurance.

Will you have enough money?

Cut costs if not.

Spend less on movies or eating out.

A **roommate** can help.

Then you can share the rent and other bills.

But it takes time to find one.

Start looking before you get a place.

Ask friends. Check the Internet.

Be safe. Always meet in person.

Look for someone who is **responsible**.

Make sure they can pay their part.

It is time to look for a place.

There are many nice areas.

But the rent may be high.

Find out before you look.

Go online. There are many free services.

Apartment Finder is one.

Look in the newspaper.

Read the **For Rent** ads.

Check at schools or churches.

They may have listings of places to rent.

Drive to areas you like.

Look for buildings with signs.

Next go see the places.

Meet with the managers.

They can give you information.

This will help you decide.

Ask about the **terms**.

The rent may be month to month.

You pay one month at a time.

And you can move out anytime.

Or there may be a **lease** to sign.

It may be for six months.

Or a year.

What utilities do you have to pay for?

Some places cover water and trash.

Most places want the first month's rent.

Some want the last month too.

Plan to pay a **deposit**.

This is money you put down.

It is used to cover any damages when you leave.

Water

Electricity

Trash

Gas

Cable

Walk around the building.

Look inside if you can.

Make sure that the place is clean.

Check the oven and refrigerator.

Turn the lights on and off.

Make sure the doors lock.

Open and close the windows.

Look for **damage**.

Ask the manager to fix it before you move in.

You may not be able to see inside.

A renter may still live there.

Find out when you can see it.

Don't agree to take it until then.

What if the place is right?

It meets all of your needs.

Then you are ready to apply.

Fill out the **application**.

Give your personal information.

The manager may call your job.

Check your **credit**.

You may not have credit yet.

Ask a parent to sign with you.

You got the place!

It's time to sign the **agreement**.

But read it first.

There is still time to ask for changes.

Make sure you know the rules.

Look for when rent is due.

Know where to pay it.

Check for fees if rent is late.

IX. MAINTENANCE – Tenant agrees to keep the Premises properly maintained and in sanitary condition during the term of the lease. Tenant must return the Premises to the same level of condition as when the day the Tenant took occupancy.

A. Tenant to keep the premises clean, sanitary, and in good condition and, upon termination of the tenancy, return the premises to Landlord in a condition identical to what existed when the Tenant took occupancy, except for ordinary wear and tear;

B. It is the Tenant's obligation to notify Landlord IMMEDIATELY of any conditions that could be hazardous in or about the Premises.

C. Tenant agrees that they will be held accountable for any damage made by guests on the Premises.

X. LANDLORD'S ACCESS – Landlord or a Landlord's representative may enter the Premises under the following conditions:

A. At anytime for the protection or preservation of the Premises.

B. After notice as required by State law for the purpose of repairing the Premises.

I. TERM – This legal document ("Hereinafter referred to as "Lease Agreement"") represents a lease agreement to begin on _____ and to continue on a

Date

month to month basis. Landlord and Tenant may modify or terminate this Lease Agreement at ANYTIME by giving _____ days' written notice.

Number of Days

II. LANDLORD & TENANT – This Lease Agreement is between

_____ (Hereinafter referred to as "Landlord")

Landlord

with mailing address of _____ City of

Street Address

_____ State of _____ Zip Code _____

City　　　　　　　　　　　　*State*　　　　　　　*Zip Code*

(Hereinafter referred to as the "Premises") to

_____ (Hereinafter referred to as "Tenant")

Tenant

III. PREMISES – The Landlord agrees to lease the premises located at

_____ City of _____ State of

Street Address　　　　　　　　　　　*City*

_____ Zip Code _____ (Hereinafter referred to as the "Premises") to

State　　　　　　*Zip Code*

Read every line.

There may be a rule about bikes.

They are not allowed on the patio.

Do you need to put your bike there?

Ask the manager to change the agreement.

Ask about the rent.

Is there a way to pay less?

Agree to stay longer than a year.

Offer to do small jobs.

Are you a student? In the military?

Ask if you can have a **discount**.

You and the manager must agree to the changes.

Then you both sign the new agreement.

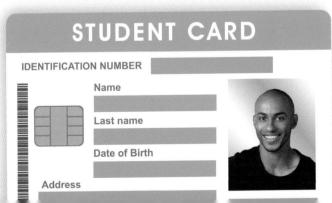

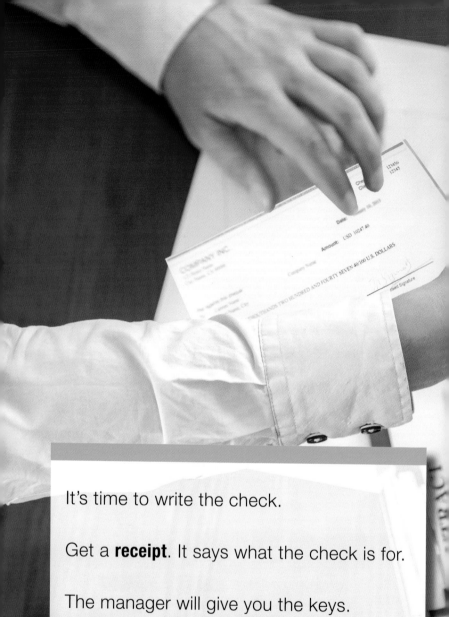

It's time to write the check.

Get a **receipt**. It says what the check is for.

The manager will give you the keys.

There is one more step.

Walk through the place.

Have the manager go with you.

Make a list of any problems.

Take pictures too.

This will protect you when you move out.

Finding your own place.

It takes time. It isn't easy.

But it's worth it.

You are taking charge.

Making your own choices.

Enjoy your **new home**!

What can go wrong when a person is looking for a place to live? Find out in *A Place of Our Own*. Want to read on?

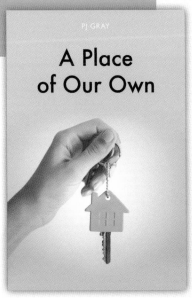

JUST *flip* THE BOOK!

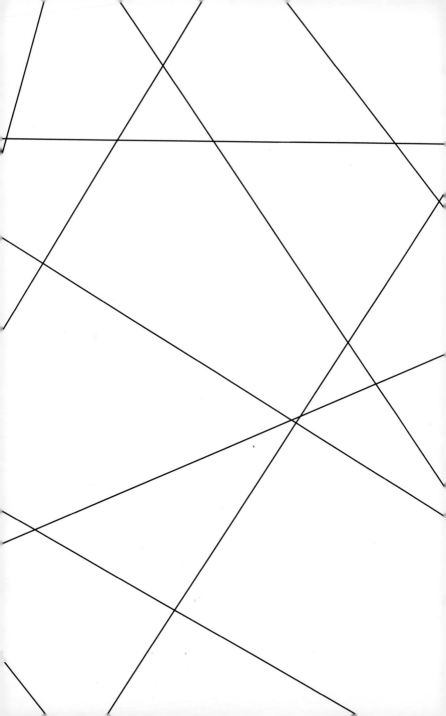

"Are you ready to move out?" Jill asked Nina. "Because I am. Let's do it!"

Nina was happy to hear this. Living with her parents was okay. But she was ready to move out. She could not afford to live alone, though.

Jill still lived with her parents too. She was also ready to move out.

Nina and Jill were best friends. The girls had finished high school last year. Now they attended a local college. They worked at the same shoe store. Both girls liked shoes. Nina liked them more. She bought a new pair whenever she could.

"We can split the rent," Nina said.

"Great," Jill said. "Remember, we need to live near school and work. I don't want to spend all day in traffic."

"Right," Nina said. "I agree. Traffic is bad."

"How do we find a place?" Jill asked.

"Let's look online," Nina said.

"Good idea," Jill said. "It's spring break soon. We can move in then. If we find a place."

Nina agreed.

Nina and Jill checked for apartments to rent. Each girl looked online. The girls shared what they found. They learned new things about each other.

Nina didn't mind spending money. She wanted to live someplace nice. Jill wanted to spend less money. She didn't care if the place wasn't perfect.

"This place is new," Nina said. "It's in the best part of town. Look, it has two bedrooms. Two bathrooms. And a pool and a gym."

Jill saw how much the rent was. "Wow!" she said. "I don't think I can afford that. Let's keep looking."

Nina was upset. She really liked the apartment. "Show me what you found," Nina said.

Jill showed Nina the online ad. "It's really cheap," Jill said.

Nina looked at the pictures. "No way," she said. "It's old. And did you see the street name?"

"Yes," Jill said. "It's on Bloom Street. So what?"

"I don't think that street is safe."

"Sure it is," Jill said.

Nina was quiet.

Jill sighed. "Let's keep looking," she said.

A few days passed.

Nina and Jill were at work. "We need to find a place fast," Jill said. "Spring break is coming. It's the only time we can move. At least until summer."

"I know," Nina said.

Their boss could hear them. "Looking for a place to live?" she asked. Nina and Jill nodded. "Do you have a plan?"

"What do you mean?" Nina asked.

"How are you looking for apartments?" she asked.

"We're looking online," Jill said.

"Did you use an apartment service?"

"No," Nina said. "Don't they charge a fee?"

"Some do," their boss said. "But others are free."

"That's a great idea," Nina said.

"The newspaper is another way. You can look at the ads," their boss said.

"I can look at my dad's paper," Jill said. "Good idea."

"Do you have a budget?" their boss asked.

Nina and Jill looked at each other. "I think so," Jill said.

Their boss smiled. She shook her head. "You need a plan," she said. "Start with a budget."

Nina and Jill met after work. They agreed on how much rent to pay.

"I don't want to pay more than that," Nina said. "I have other bills."

"I agree," Jill said. "That's all I can afford too."

Then they decided on the location. The location was nice. But it was not the most expensive neighborhood. It was affordable. School and work were nearby.

"Let's look in that part of town," Jill said.

"Okay," Nina said. "That's a safe area."

The girls met with an apartment service. It gave them a lead. The apartment was a little over budget. But it was near school.

Nina and Jill made an appointment. They went to the apartment. The manager was there. The girls looked inside. It was very nice. There was new carpet. "Look, Jill," Nina said. "The carpet matches my shoes."

Jill smiled. She kept looking around.

"Two bedrooms. Two bathrooms," Nina said. "And it's close to school and work."

Jill wanted to look at more places.

"It's new. The space is big and so nice," Nina said. "Let's get it! Please."

"All right," Jill said. "We'll do it."

They were ready to sign the lease. "This is a one-year lease," the manager said. "We need your first month's rent. And a deposit in the same amount."

"What?" Nina asked. "So you want two month's rent now?"

"Yes," the manager said. "The deposit plus the first month's rent. We also have other fees. It's all here on paper."

Jill looked at Nina. "We didn't know about the deposit. It will take all our savings," Jill said. "We still need money for food."

"And the electric bill," Nina said.

"And our car payments," Jill said. "And gas!"

"And my shoe budget," Nina said. "I will not give that up!"

They left the rental office with a new plan. The girls needed more money to rent a place. Money for the deposit. Plus rent money. They agreed to look for a cheaper apartment. A place they could afford.

Jill found a great apartment in the newspaper. It was a good deal. The rent was cheap. It was larger. School was blocks away. And so was work.

They looked at the apartment. It was old and a little shabby.

"It's very big," Jill said to Nina. "And we can walk to school and work. It will save us money on gas."

Nina looked down. The carpet was dirty. It was worn out in places. And it smelled like smoke and wet dog.

The manager showed them more rooms. There were metal bars on the bedroom windows.

Jill looked up. There was a big stain on the ceiling. "What is that?" she asked.

"Just an old leak from the roof," he said. "It's been fixed."

Nina was not happy.

"Can we rent one month at a time?" Jill asked.

"What?" he asked.

"Do you offer a monthly lease?" Jill asked.

"No," the manager said. "Our leases are for two years."

"Two years?" Jill gasped.

Nina looked at Jill. "Let's get out of here," she said.

Nina and Jill were upset. A week had passed. The girls had looked online. They had tried an apartment service. And checked the newspaper. But there weren't any good deals in their target location. And time was running out.

Nina had a day off. Jill asked her to keep looking for apartments. "I'll try," Nina said. "I have to go to my aunt's house. It's her birthday." Nina's aunt lived near their school and work.

Nina arrived at her aunt's front door. She rang the doorbell and waited. Nina turned away from the door. She looked across the street. There was a brick house.

Nina saw a woman in the front window. The woman was putting up a sign. It said For Rent.

Nina stared. Then her aunt opened the door. "Happy birthday!" Nina said. "Do you know who lives across the street? In that house."

Nina's aunt told her all about the woman. "She has a second-floor apartment. She rents it out," her aunt said.

"Does she rent to college kids?" Nina asked.

"I'm not sure," her aunt said. "But I think she likes quiet tenants."

Nina kissed her aunt. "Be right back," Nina said. "I'm going across the street. I have to meet that woman."

Nina ran across the street. She knocked on the door of the brick house. A woman answered. The woman's name was Mrs. Davis.

"Are your renting an apartment?" Nina asked. "I saw your sign in the window. My aunt lives across the street."

"Yes," Mrs. Davis said. "It's the upstairs unit. Would you like to see it now?"

They went upstairs to see the apartment. It was so nice. Nina dialed Jill's number. "You have to see this place," Nina said.

"I get off work in an hour," Jill said.

Nina gave her the address.

"My dad works nearby," Jill said. "That's a good area. It's very safe."

Nina waited for Jill. She passed the time with her aunt. Then Jill texted. She was waiting outside.

Nina and Jill went to see Mrs. Davis. The apartment was a good size. There were two large bedrooms. But there was no dining room. They could live with that.

It was very clean and in good shape. It was not far from school or work. And it was below their budget. But there was one problem. It had only one bathroom.

"Will you be okay with that?" Jill asked Nina.

"I think so," Nina said. "What about you?"

"Yes," Jill said. "But we'll have to make a bathroom schedule."

"The kitchen is new," Mrs. Davis said.

"Is there off-street parking?" Nina asked.

"Yes," Mrs. Davis said. "For a monthly fee. You can park in one of the spots in the alley."

Jill looked at Nina. She wanted to act fast. "How long is the lease?" Jill asked.

"Six months," Mrs. Davis said. "But you pay for your electricity and heat."

"We'll sign a one-year lease," Jill said.

Nina looked at Jill. What was Jill doing?

Jill went on. "But we want free heat and electricity," she said. "And one of those alley parking spots for free."

Nina was shocked. She did not want Jill to mess this up.

Mrs. Davis looked at them. She paused. "Free heat," Mrs. Davis said. "And new carpets and ceiling fans."

Jill looked at Nina. Nina nodded. "Where do we sign?" Jill asked.

They shook hands with Mrs. Davis. "I will have the lease ready tomorrow. Fill out this application. Be ready to pay a deposit. Plus your first month's rent."

Nina and Jill hugged. Then they walked to
their cars. "You were amazing!" Nina said.

"Thanks," Jill said.

"Why did you try to make a deal?"

Jill smiled. "I just kept thinking of your shoe budget."

Could Nina and Jill have found a place to live faster? Want to learn more about how to find the right place?

LIFESKILLS IN ACTION

LIVING SKILLS+

Finding A Place To Live

CARRIE GWYNNE

JUST *flip* THE BOOK!